# DOU

Douglas first took to the a
*White Horse Inn* for the P;
Sydney, Australia. It wasn't .
preferred working behind-the-scenes in marketing and publicity,
and eventually in producing musicals.

For the next ten years, he produced shows, established theatre
groups and had a finger in all aspects of production, including the
occasional onstage cameo when a silent walk-on part beckoned.

At age 22, he commissioned and professionally staged the full-
length concert musical version of Mike Batt's *The Hunting Of The
Snark* and launched the first show by Australian comedy duo
*The Umbilical Brothers*. He toured a series of one-man shows and
helped to develop several new musicals.

In 1994/5 he was a co-producer of one of the world's first amateur
productions of *Les Miserables*, which ran for 42 performances
with over 40,000 people attending the show.

Based in London, Douglas was Editor of *Amateur Stage
Magazine* (www.amateurstagemagazine.co.uk) for five years.
He continues to stimulate interest in amateur theatre and
encourages development of modern theatre practice through his
freelance articles. His first book *Packed To the Rafters*, was an
enormous success and has been used by groups world-wide keen
to increase the size of their audiences.

He is currently working on the launch of www.britishtheatre.com
amongst other things.

# PACKED TO THE RAFTERS 2

## 2013 Edition

How to market your theatre group and show using social networks and online marketing.

A guide for school, amateur and fringe theatre.

# Douglas Mayo

**SILVERMOON PUBLISHING**
London
www.silvermoonpublishing.co.uk

# PACKED TO THE RAFTERS 2

First published in Great Britain in December 2013
by Silvermoon Publishing
3rd Floor, 207 Regent Street, London, W1B 3HH

Author photograph by www.actorheadshots.co.uk
Typeset by Silvermoon Publishing

A CIP catalogue record for this book is available
from the British Library.

ISBN 978 1 84094 908 7

*For Judy & Jim.*
*"Don't just talk about it - Do it!"*

# Contents

**What next!**

# Acknowledgements

It's worth repeating that you can read a lot of books, but a lot of the learning comes from the doing. There have been many successes and failures along the way, but most of the outcomes arose from the efforts applied in PR and marketing. I learned the hard way, that you disregard its importance at your peril.

I need to thank Julian Cound for pushing me to write this one. Julian remains a common sense marketing guy from his groups Darlington Operatic Society. I could have asked for no finer person to have taken my place as Editor of Amateur Stage.

Thanks also to Ian Hornby, who has encouraged me to pass on as much information about marketing as possible. His passion for amateur theatre and his encouragement of newcomers should be a template for us all.

To the many people who helped me to promote shows and helped me learn the "How To" by doing it for real. Thank you.

Special thanks to Phil Matthews who after I finished the first book insisted that this one needed to be written.

# INTRODUCTION

Over the past 5 years, Social networking has become an institutionalised part of marketing all over the world. To try to promote anything without harnessing the power of social networks is likely to prove a frustrating and ultimately less than successful experience.

No other singular marketing method other than direct mail and email has caught the imagination of the public and the marketeers on such a scale. It is not uncommon now to find corporations investing huge amounts of money into their social network activities and appointing teams of people to track and take advantage of the myriad opportunities presented by these networks.

I'm writing this book as an introduction to social networking. I realised that the amateur and fringe theatre community needed a basic how to guide to get them started, showing some tips and tricks and explaining how social networks could help them spread the word about their group and their shows. Don't let the idea of social networking daunt you, you can easily achieve some great results and promote your group without incurring any sleepless nights or becoming a slave to your computer.

Social networking was once solely the domain of Facebook and Twitter but has recently come to include a lot of other sites including You Tube, Tumblr, Pinterest, Google +, and Flickr to name but a few. In this book I will primarily focus on Facebook and Twitter and will briefly touch on the others. My reason for this is simple, I honestly believe that your time is best spent in arenas which will give you the greatest return for time invested and arenas which represent the marketplace you are trying to attract. It is my belief, that at this time Facebook and Twitter represent the best return for the investment of your time and effort and handled correctly those two platforms alone could significantly improve your visibility and selling potential online.

Carrying on from one of the points made in my first book, Packed To the Rafters 1, no man is an island and no one man a publicity machine makes. Always try to get a few helpers on your pr team. It's a great way to get additional involvement from some of the younger members of your group.

So, don't be daunted. I'll be trying to keep the concept and principles outlines as clear as possible.

The nature of social networks means that they are constantly changing and adapting to new ideas and concepts. Processes outlined in this book relate to the basic operating systems of both Twitter and Facebook and the underlying philosophy that both operate under. Therefore, whilst the added extras they offer might differ in a year from now all of the basic concepts contained in this book should still be operational and of use to you in your promotional campaigns (I hope you are listening Mr Zuckerberg)!

Right, grab a cup of coffee, and digest the next few chapters before you even get close to a computer. To be successful with social networking you need to fully understand how it all works from a theoretical point of view and to understand the concepts that will make it work for you.

**Get In Touch**

Social media is by its very nature a two-way conversation, and I really want to hear from you!

You can connect with me online and give me your feedback on this and my previous book. Tell me if there's something I missed, or something you'd like clarified for future editions of the book. Given the speed at which social networks develop this book will doubtless be updated yearly so your feedback is essential.

*Douglas Mayo*
*London, 2013*

**Here's how you find me**

**Website**
www.packedrafterspr.co.uk

**Twitter**
@packedrafterspr

**Facebook**
www.facebook.com/packedtotherafterspr

**LinkedIn**
http://uk.linkedin.com/pub/douglas-mayo/64/835/83a/

or **email me**
doug@packedrafterspr.co.uk

# 1. SOCIAL NETWORKING AND THEATRE

It is my personal opinion that Social networking works particularly well with all things theatre.

Theatre is an incredibly visual media. If your group can muster great pictures, and look at accessing and posting great video clips via websites such as You Tube, you can create an incredibly vibrant social network. Best of all you have potentially hundred of audience members who you can involve.

To get an idea of just how the professional theatre marketing teams do it, hunt around a website like Facebook for the current hit West End shows. Take a look at what they are doing and see if anything could be adapted to your own purposes.

For example, take a look at the Facebook page for Wicked (www.facebook.com/WickedUK), it's a mix of great photos, cast information, and other events designed to keep you coming back for more.

By browsing around the platform you are intending to use be it Facebook, Twitter etc. you can get an idea of what techniques work and what techniques don't. Why spend time trying to re-invent the wheel. West End shows spend a fortune each week developing their social media platforms. Take their lead and use some of their techniques. By all means try some of your own but in the long term, using tried and tested techniques that you see on their pages will save you time and ensure great results.

## 2. HOW SOCIAL NETWORKING HAS CHANGED THE WAY WE MARKET OURSELVES

Dismissed in their early stages as websites where kids hung out, the development of social networking has been remarkable and quick by relative standards.

Today, more than 1.1 billion people use Facebook each month, with 500 million account on Twitter and 50 million using newcomer Tumblr. No matter which way you look at it, social networking is a phenomenon that is unlikely to go away any time soon.

The most important thing to consider when you look at social networking is how the "middle man" is no longer of importance. When I refer to the "middle man", I am talking about the television channel, newspaper or magazine proprietor or the radio station. These "middle men" used to determine what was said or written and if they did not deem it to be important various stories and messages were normally ignored. Social networking changed the way media works in a drastic way by allowing everyday people to bypass the gatekeepers and set the topics of conversation.

Today it is quick and easy to share information and links with a large number of people via social networks without involving traditional media. There is no doubt that information backed by the recommendation of someone you know carries extra weight.

It is a fact now that almost every credible business today has a social media presence. Many of my associates carry out a Facebook search as part of research for upcoming features and many will use it as a way of accessing information about certain theatre groups when websites are out of date or unavailable.

Its is true in the current climate to say that people interact more with each other more often online than they do in real life. It's a world where terms like "tweeting", "trending", "friending" and "unfriending" are now commonly used in everyday speech.

Social networking is brilliant in that it offers users instant gratification. In previous years a theatre group wishing to publicise their shows would have to arrange an interview, have photos taken and processed and then wait for a paper or magazine to come out often 3-4 weeks later. With social networking you can have your news and information available to a mass audience in a few hours and modify your message right up to the day of performance to take into consideration any empty seats you have to sell. Social networks offer a last minute route to selling tickets at a discount or re-enforcing your message right up until the last night of your season.

### The Biggest Misnomer

Before we go any further let me make one thing clear. SELL, SELL, SELL may be the language of direct mail, the village marketplace or phone selling but it is not the language of social networking. If you are a social network user you will know what I mean by this. Nothing irritates me more than having people 'sell at me'.

When approaching social networking, think about engaging your audience not working the hard sell. The most successful groups online have their audience do all the work for them. Do you job right and your social network "friends" will make sure that you are rewarded. In the true meaning of viral marketing, a good social networking campaign encouraging engagement with your audience will spread like wildfire putting your offering indirectly in front of many more people than you could possibly imagine.

For instance, a Facebook page with just under 1000 Likes can have a posting seen by over 17,000 people within a 24-hour period. That's not bad for a few minutes work. It's even better when your posting gets people responding online with a positive discussion ensuing. As a customer, there's a strange satisfaction in interacting with your favourite theatre group. It gives the patron a feeling of ownership and more often than not a feeling that their thoughts are valued and important to the group.

A great social marketing campaign will make your audience feel like they have a connection with you, but be warned you will also open the doorway to them telling you if something isn't quite up to scratch. Don't ignore criticism but acknowledge it and if possible do something about it. Your clients are telling you how to keep their support, it's not an attack.

A survey of many Facebook pages owned by theatre groups will show pages full of sell, sell, sell messages and I can guarantee such messages fall on deaf ears after the first one or two. The challenge to any social networker is finding a way to engage your audience and get your sales message across without the hard sell approach. It's not terribly difficult and in engaging your audience you get loyalty, support and the all-important word of mouth so vital to any campaign.

# 3. MARKETING YOUR GROUP OR SHOW ONLINE – THE BASICS

When it comes to online marketing and social media don't just dive in and hope for the best. Take a moment to think about your group, what you are trying to promote and what you hope to achieve in the long run. Just because everyone you know has an account with Pinterest, doesn't mean that you should too. Like any form of marketing, it's essential that you identify your potential market, identify where that market exists – that is, what forms of social media do they use?, and based on that information you can then work out what sort of tools you need to approach your potential audience.

## Why Online?

When I started marketing shows back in Sydney we relied on photocopiers, the postage service, posters, flyers, community flyering, you name it we did it. Online marketing and social networking though have made the job of the press and marketing team a little bit easier, although at the same time they have given you the tools to broadcast to such a large number of people that sometimes your message gets lost in the throng.

Just consider this though, there are billions of people online and some of them are your ideal patrons. Your website and social networking pages are like a store in a shopping mall but you are always open for business. Even when your team is sleeping, your promotional messages continue to filter through the system and reach people that you could never have reached before.

With this form of marketing the idea is to broadcast your message far and wide, attract your audience in and then capture their details or have them join your network so that you can engage them in specific niche broadcasts that will hopefully appeal to them.

**Why it works?**

A few things to consider. Online marketing is:-

• **Effective** – In this modern age people spend a lot of time online. Whether employers like it or not Facebook and Twitter have become a common part of the work-place. Next time you are on public transport look at how many people are using their mobile devices to link to social networks or read email.

• **Affordable** – Most theatre groups like the idea of social networking because at a basic level it's FREE. Sure, you can enhance your offering and your reach with a small budget but if you have nothing you can still do well.

• **Real** – Online marketing tools and social media thrives in many cases on a personal touch. You and your theatre group are not some huge multi national conglomerate and that can work in your favour. Keep your online campaigns personal and real, your audiences are more likely to engage with you because they see you as being real people that they know and hopefully trust.

Let me just ask you this. As someone who is on the internet, how much time do you spend looking at websites, interacting with interest groups you've found on Facebook or Twitter, or emailing friends you've discovered online with mutual interests?

Social networking and online marketing should bring your group several benefits:-

## 1. Drive traffic to your website.
Your website is the major hub of your group, and everything you do should be aimed at driving traffic to it. Make sure your website is up to date, make sure you can sell tickets from your site, make it easy for potential members and patrons to contact you. I know its sounds rudimentary but you would be surprised how many amateur websites I've seen where there is no email address or contact details.

## 2. New ways to connect.
By establishing a presence on social networks that your potential audience uses, you'll become visible to a whole new set of potential patrons.

## 3. Build trust.
People will always prefer to do business with people they know. Social networking and your online presence gives your patrons, sponsors and potential new members a chance to get to know you.

## 4. Start a conversation
Social networking is not a one-way medium. Anyone who thinks they can stand up with a megaphone and start broadcasting is sorely mistaken. Two-way discussions will return you far greater results.

## 5. Create something of value.
Part of the secret of marketing online or building a large social network is creating useful content and giving it away.

If you can create a useful resource or interesting content targeted at your market, they will keep coming back for more.

## 6. Provide timely, up-to-date information.

It's not longer acceptable to find out news a week after it happens. With social networking and online marketing it's possible to build suspense and interest around important announcements. You can also build a following with people who want accurate information first. Make sure you co-ordinate your pr team to make sure that any important information is placed on your website and on social media networks at the same time.

## 7. Data capture

Building a database or group of online followers is key to the success of your campaigns. Once people have seen your shows, become a part of your online communities or engaged with you in any way they are more likely to come and see a show or spread the word to other people. That list is like gold and should be valued. As your list grows it follows that the chances of selling out your next show grows incrementally.

## 8. Market research

More than ever before you'll be able to talk to your audiences and get feedback on all manner of questions without is costing you a fortune. Best of all, those audiences will feel more a part of your endeavours because you have bothered to ask them what they think. One thing though, if you ask a question, be prepared to take the feedback on board. If your audience tells you something, you ignore it at your peril.

# 4. NO IS A WORD I DON'T WANT TO HEAR!

I've mentioned some of the concepts in this book to friends and theatre groups around the UK, and in some cases their first words are NO we can't do that, or NO we won't be allowed to do that. They then tell me, in an informed manner ,that their theatre won't let them, the rights holders won't allow it or their committees will say No.

The biggest thing to note with most of these suggestions is that none of them bother to ask or make an enquiry. Amateur theatre for years has been living under a great big cloud of negativity, with a fear of change that would fill many psychiatry textbooks with case studies.

Times are changing and social media is just one of those changes. In many cases the technology is moving faster than the people who use it, or the organisations who seek to harness its potential.

What groups need to realise is that there's no harm in asking.

Think about this, most rights holders in the UK, especially for musicals are paid a percentage of your gross box office receipts. The more you make – the more they make. It's a simple equation, which is so often overlooked. For years, certain organisations have put the fear of God into groups making them afraid to rock the boat or try something new. It's become apparent to me though in my dealings with people, that they would love you to ask questions or suggest new things.

Chances are when you ask a question, someone else may have beaten you to it. The answer you get may not be the one you want, but it is also possible that with a slight amendment to your plan, you can so something remarkable with your social networks that will help sell those extra seats.

So, make sure, before you rubbish the ideas contained within, or any brainstorms had by your committee, or PR team, that you will take time to ask questions, find out what can be done and wherever possible, try a new idea. Just try one per production – how could that hurt?

Just don't just say NO!

## 5. WHERE DO YOU BEGIN?

The world of social networking and online marketing is vast. So many different websites and forums exist so where do you start?

Perhaps, the first thing you need to realise is that you don't need to rush out and use everything. Take a look at the various tools and then pick and chose according to your needs. Build your social networks one by one – as you become more and more comfortable with one, start looking at how another might work in tandem with your existing efforts.

New networks and tools will become available and at times you'll feel like it is physically impossible to keep up with social networking trends. In the words of Douglas Adams 'DON'T PANIC'. It is more important to look at your approach to your challenges, than to worry yourself with the tools. If you have a sound marketing strategy, you can apply it to whatever tools come along. I would go so far as to say that you really don't need to be ahead of the curve when it comes to new networks or tools. It is probably better that you lag behind a bit. Why invest your time and effort in a new social network that may disappear (as many have) in a few short months. As a general rule if your customers aren't using a social network, then don't bother with it.

What is important throughout though is your theatre group, your show, your passions and your ideas. It is more important to have a message, some great content and some creativity. You can learn the rest as you go along.

25

**Your online marketing plan.**

Let's not waste valuable time. Take some time now to draw up a quick online marketing plan. It doesn't need to be too complicated but you need to address a few questions:-

**1. What are my marketing aims and objectives?**
What do you hope to achieve using social networking and online marketing? More audiences, greater awareness? Think carefuly about what you want to achieve so you know if you've been successful. These could include raising awareness of your brand, increasing sales, building an email list.

**2. Who is my target market?**
Know your audience! If you are staging the White Horse Inn – you target market certainly isn't 18-22 year olds. Be realistic in who you need to approach and know what value you can offer the audience you wish to attract. Think about what you offer that is unique. What would your ideal customer look like? For forward planning ask who your future audience might be. Theatre is a dynamic sector. Audiences need to be developed. Target all your efforts at an older demographic and you may find that you will outlast them!

**3. Where can I find them?**
Where does your market 'hang out'? Use the search function on social media platforms to locate your potential audience. Some hot tips for finding your audience online include:-
• Do a **Google search** to find blogs or websites in your area of interest.
• Use **keywords** relevant to your production or service

(eg amateur theatre, York) on social networks. Are there Linked In groups, Google + Communities or Facebook Groups built around a topic that is relevant to your theatre group. Use the Twitter Directory (www.wefollow.com) to find the top Twitter accounts in your area.

## 4. Which tools should I use?
Which tools will reach your market and allow you to manage them given your resources and time availability? There are so many tools available, it is sometimes hard to know where to start. Keep in mind though at the centre of everything you do is your website – it is the hub of your online marketing. The ultimate aim of your marketing efforts is to drive people here to join your mailing list, become aware of your group, and hopefully buy a ticket.

Another key aim is to build an email marketing list. Your email newsletter will provide specific calls to action leading people to buy from you, and in most cases it will also drive patrons to your website.

## 5. How to measure your results?
How will you know if you are successful? Will your results be measured in ticket sales, mailing list sign ups etc? Getting results with online marketing and social networks can take time so don't give up. Be patient. If something clearly isn't working though, drop it and look at other methods. You'll get a clearer feel for these things as you go along.

# 6. CALLS TO ACTION

Although one of the most basic principles of marketing ,'Calls To Action' are often ignored by PR and marketing teams.

You've spent a lot of time and effort to get people to your website, so make sure you tell them what you want them to do when they get there. Calls to action may include:-

1. Sign up to your email newsletter
2. Visit a website
3. Become a fan on Facebook or a Follower on Twitter
4. Buy a ticket
5. Enter a competition
6. Leave a comment

BUT, whatever you do don't confuse people by using too many Calls To Action. If you do they may do none of them!

# 7. THE SOCIAL NETWORKS – HOW TO CHOOSE THEM AND USE THEM

Andy Warhol once said that in his lifetime everyone would get his or her 15 minutes of fame. I am sure that he'd revise this statement if he'd been alive to see the advent of social networks. More than any other development in the last twenty years (reality TV included), social networking has made everyone a celebrity. Whether you are a business or an individual, if you have a personality and a brand to communicate, you can build an army of loyal fans.

A simple journey through the indexes at You Tube will show you a new brand of media celebrity emerging. Twin 19 year olds (Channel – JacksGap) who command viewing audiences of millions, are now the youth equivalent of GMTV.

To be successful on social networks you need three things as a business, they are influence, profile and reach. More than ever before social networks make it possible for anyone to achieve this by giving you the ability to publish your own content online. Content is the starting point for everything. Social networks and online marketing is how you disseminate that content and get the word out to the world at large.

We are about to take a quick look at the principles of social networking, that you can apply to whichever of the networks you choose to utilise. Whilst it is impossible to say what lies just around the corner, the networks that seem to be predominant now and which I feel may best serve your interests include Facebook, LinkedIn, Twitter, Google+, You Tube and Pinterest and we'll take a more detailed look at these in future chapters.

**Most social networks share a few common features:-**
1. They allow you to create a personal profile with some information about yourself;

2. They allow you to update your 'status' – a short description of what you are doing;

3. They allow you to 'Tag' your content to show your location;

4. They allow you to set up special interest groups, lists of pages to share that are of interest with others;

5. They allow you to add friends and followers to your lists of contacts or allow you to follow others.

6. They allow you to create and manage events;

7. They allow you to add and share video and photos;

8. They allow you to extend your reach, promoting your product or service through advertising.

Whilst originally the domain of individuals, most businesses quickly realised that the networks offered a huge opportunity to promote their products through marketing. Most of the social networks responded in turn by building business features into their systems, making it easier for businesses to get their message out.

Perhaps the best statistic when it comes to social networks is that about a fifth to one-third of the time people spend online, is spent on social networks (Source: Nielsen Media).

That statistic is expected in, crease substantially due to the introduction of smartphones that allow users to constantly monitor their social networks.

# 8. THE SALES FUNNEL

The sales funnel visually describes the sales process from initial contact to final sale. It uses the metaphor of a leaky funnel, into which a seller can "drop" sales opportunities. At some point, sales opportunities are removed from the funnel because potential customers become uninterested or you determine their lack of fit.

**Stages of the sales funnel.**

The stages of a sales process refer to a potential customer's degree of readiness to commit to a deal (from the seller's perspective). Or put in a different way, readiness may be seen as the probability of the sale taking place.

As a sales opportunity moves down the funnel, time to closing decreases and the probability of the sale occurring increases. The sales funnel metaphor enables you to analyse and manage a portfolio of sales opportunities.

**Mechanics of the sales funnel.**

In the process of pursuing a sales opportunity, you essentially work to remove barriers to the sale. When you remove a barrier, the opportunity moves to the next stage. Barriers include uncertainty about your product's fit and value, lack of budget or the customer's buying process.

As you gain experience in working with customers and sales processes, you can create your own version of the sales funnel, complete with specific steps and actions to move prospects from stage to stage. What we have described here can act as a starting point or template.

## Stages in the sales funnel

**Lead** (Suspect): A lead (also known as a suspect) is someone you have not spoken to. But if a lead appears similar in profile to your target customer, you may decide that they are worth pursuing. Track your most fruitful sources of leads (i.e., leads that become customers). For example, where did your patrons find you? newpaper, radio etc.

**Prospect:** A prospect has confirmed interest in your offering. You have had a conversation, provided the person with information about what you do or have they visited your website, and both of you have agreed to a next step in the sales process.

**Qualified prospect:** Qualification is the most critical and demanding stage of the sales funnel. In the qualification process, you verify that the prospect has a need for your product, that the prospect sees value in your offering, that there is sufficient budget for a deal, that you have access to the decision-maker, and that there is an agreed-upon timeline for the sales process.

**Committed:** Ideally, you want to close the deal when all red flags have been dealt with. In reality, most deals close while critical red flags still exist. At this point, you have provided the customer with a proposal that outlines key contractual terms. When a customer has agreed to move forward with a deal, they are "committed" (also known as "verbal commitment" or "verbal"). What remains is to work out the details of the contract, delivery and payment, all of which have the potential to "undo" the commitment. The commitment may be offered contingent upon certain terms being met.

**Transacted**: A sale has transpired when a contract is signed by both parties or a ticket purchased. From a salesperson's perspective, the fulfilment of the contract is the responsibility of other parts of the organization, and the salesperson can now focus on the next opportunity. In the case of early-stage start-ups, however, frequently the person that sells is also involved in fulfilling the contract.

## The leaky funnel

If a sales opportunity does not move down the funnel, the sale will not happen and the opportunity should be removed, hence the "leaky" funnel. A leaky funnel is not necessarily bad; as a salesperson, you want to focus on opportunities that are likely to yield results. It is the nature of sales to have to remove an opportunity from your funnel. It does not mean that you will not sell to that account (a positive action by the customer can put them back into the funnel), but for the time being, you should centre your attention on opportunities that remain in the funnel.

Well that's the theory. In theatre things are just a tiny bit different. Obviously our intent is to get people to buy tickets. In doing so sometimes we will never have any person-to-person interaction with our patrons. We need to remove all impediments to patrons buying tickets and these can be sizeable with amateur theatre groups. From my study of groups these can include:-

## 1. Location and availability of ticketing outlets
It is incredibly difficult for modern day working people to

buy tickets from a high street location during 9am to 5pm working hours. Most people will not go out of their way to buy using this method. Likewise, phone operating hours that include 2pm to 5pm Mon – Thurs where patrons are faced with engaged phones if they are able to call at all, will likewise lose you sales. Ideally, you want your patrons to be able to buy a ticket 24 hours a day, 7 days a week, with the introduction of online ticketing, groups can now sell tickets in their sleep. Don't underestimate the number of people who plan their entertainment at 11pm at night when the kids are asleep and they finally have a peaceful moment alone with their computers. Do you really want to lose those sales because the patrons can't buy when they want. There is no doubt in my mind that if you then make them wait or have to jump through difficult hoops to get a ticket they will abandon you for something simpler.

## 2. Payment methods

Many groups still encourage mail bookings by cheque or postal order. It worked for many years during the direct mail boom where people would blindly send off for goods advertised in magazines, but most consumers are now slightly more savvy. Also be aware that the era of cheque books is nearly at an end. It won't be immediate but a quick poll of people in your group will show you just how fast they are disappearing. If you are looking to attract younger audiences, you'll soon find most don't have a cheque book and don't have time to queue at a post office for a postal order just for the 'privilege' of seeing your show.

## 3. Seating allocation

Most patrons in modern society would like to pick where they sit. Look at any online or telephone system for booking any sort of seat now, whether it be airline, cinema or theatre and nearly EVERY system offers you a chance to select where you want to sit. People with sight or hearing impediments can choose to sit closer to the stage whilst others may prefer aisle seating. Some may have their favourite seats in your auditorium. With modern systems it is not a great problem to offer your patrons the ability to choose where they want to sit.

### 4. Finding information about your show

Somebody at work has told you that there's a great amateur group staging The King & I near you, but you don't know the details. Most computer literate people will try to Google you, or use social networks to get information and book. If your group isn't on Facebook or Twitter and doesn't have an up-to-date website you have in most cases instantly lost a sale. Potential patrons need to be able to find you using online methods and be able to book when they want not when it suits you. It doesn't matter that your committee has never seen a social network and doesn't use them. A quick poll amongst your friends (remember it's usually they who buy your tickets) will show you that 80% of the general population are online and part of the social network/online phenomenon.

In most circumstances you want the theatre ticket sales process reduced to as few steps as possible:-

See flyer – Go Online – Buy tickets

Google details – go to website – buy tickets

Google details – go to website – invite friends – buy tickets

Anything more than four steps probably means a lost sale as your potential patrons attention span may drift elsewhere.

Immediacy is everything.

## Building Community

Where social networks come into their-own most of the time, is that they allow your group to build a community around your group or your show. The most important thing when looking at marketing your group is to work out your audience and tailor your offering to them. It is not about you. Sure you probably do amateur theatre because you get something out of it, but in this part of the process it's all about your audience – your feelings have little currency. In this part of the deal what you are offering is akin to a community service and everything you do must be approached with that in mind.

Approached with care and with planning, social networks will help you find your audience. It will help you to build a reputation, it will help you build a list of your patrons, it will build word of mouth about what you do and it will build trust with your audience. All-in-all the end result should see patrons returning to see more of your shows and see your tickets sell.

# 9. WHICH NETWORK SHOULD I USE?

Just for ease of identification this is the list of the top 10 social networks rates in terms of registered users in 2013.

## Facebook
www.facebook.com
Users: 1 billion +
Facebook is the largest and most geographically spread general social network. Look at setting up a 'Page' on Facebook to promote your group.

## Twitter
www.twitter.com
Users: 600 million +
Twitter continues to grow as a network. It's important and influential because more than most networks it operates in real-time.

## Google+
http://plus.google.com
Users: 500 million +
Introduced in 2011, Google+ integrates its previous social services with new features.

## Habbo
www.habbo.com
Users: 268 million +
Habbo is a general social networking site for teenagers. It currently operates in over 31 communities worldwide.

## LinkedIn
www.linkedin.com
Users: 225 million +
LinkedIn is a business oriented social network. A combination of CV/Resume and business contacts, you can also set up company pages and create groups.

## Instagram
http://instagram.com
Users: 130 million +
A photo sharing / smartphone app/ social network. A great place to share image based content.

## Bebo
www.bebo.com
Users: 117 million +
A social network with a younger demographic.

## Pinterest
http://pinterest.com
Users: 70 million +
Pinterest is a pinboard-style social bookmarking site based on images that are pinned from websites onto themed boards.

## MySpace
www.myspace.com
Users: 50 million +
Yes for those of you who've been online for a while MySpace is still operating. Pre-Facebook, MySpace was the king of social networks. It's now set itself up as a network for music and other creative work and boasts Justin Timberlake as one of its major backers.

### YouTube
www.youtube.com
Users: Over a million watching 6 billion hours of video each month

Not generally considered a social network, I tend to disagree and include You Tube in my list of networks to consider when it comes to promoting your content. This comes with some caveats though. The filming of theatre is fraught with rules and regulations and you must take ALL of these into consideration when using You Tube.

There are also several local UK directories to think about when it comes to amateur theatre. The two largest are:-

### Amateur Stage
www.amateurstagemagazine.co.uk
Users: - 2,400 +
Blog about your shows, list your shows in the online diary, submit pictures and videos, create a page for your group or special interest subject.

### Amdram
www.amdram.co.uk
Users:- 3,900+
Set up a profile for yourself and your group, list your upcoming shows, create posts.

### So which networks should I join?

A good guiding principle is to focus on the largest networks and perhaps something local to you that targets your niche.

If you are new to networking, start with Facebook and Twitter but consider:-

• Set up a Facebook page and a Twitter account. They are the major industry players and it makes sense for people to try to find you here. It makes sense that with such large user numbers, there will be a lot of people who will find what you have to offer of interest. You can also link some of the other social networking sites directly to your Facebook and Twitter accounts such as your blog and Instagram or Pinterest images.

• If you work on the business side of your group, it would be a good idea to set up a profile on LinkedIn. LinkedIn is a great place to source business contacts and can help you when it comes to potential sponsors or other local business contacts.

• Sign up to Google+ if only to benefit from better search results on Google.

• Use Pinterest if you are able to generate a strong visual image to your group. Does your group use a great photographer to photograph rehearsals and your shows. They get on Pinterest and share those pictures. Pinterest is a huge source of referral traffic to your website.

• If you want to attract younger audiences then look at Bebo or Habbo but be careful. If looking at these networks ask someone in your group who is age appropriate to run that network for you. There's nothing worse than having an older person trying to be hip to younger audiences. I'm sure you know what I mean. You wouldn't want your dad dancing with you in the disco!

Take some time to think about your next step too. Start with one or two but if you think that some of the other networks have potential future interest go and register with them now, if only to register and hold a user name. Registering usernames on social networking sites is a bit like registering domain names. If you don't register it someone else may do it before you.

Take time to consider what you will call your social networks. This might depend on how you are best known, your group name, or even be based on a topic but ultimately think about how people who are looking for you will try to find you. Try to keep your usernames constant across the platforms. For instance, my Facebook username is packedrafterspr and my Twitter handle is @ packedrafterspr. Try to avoid to many abbreviations using a user name like KAODS will cause confusion and make searching for you difficult. Kilvenyamateurdramatics may work better. Just take a bit of time to think about it, you want people to find you easily.

### A little local networking

As amateur theatre groups we are all about our local communities, so let's get that aspect of the social networking experience working to our advantage. Most groups could benefit from the concept of 'tagging'. Many of you do it now without even thinking of the applications for your theatre groups.

Most social networks including Facebook, Twitter, Google+ and Instagram allow you to show other people where you are. You show people that you are seeing a show, attending rehearsals or auditions. These little plugs are great ways to re-enforce your involvement and prod potential patrons. You can also use a specific location-based network like Foursquare (http://foursquare.com). You can register with

Foursquare as a business and offer other users special offers or information on events in their area. I know of one local group who use Foursquare to promote return visitors as Foursquare register the number of times you visit and reward you with titles based on your usage. You can become the Mayor of your theatre just by logging in every time you attend. It's novel and fun way of getting your audiences involved on another level.

# 10. HOW TO EFFECTIVELY MANAGE YOUR SOCIAL NETWORKS

Whether you decide to use two networks or number of networks, it could be worthwhile utilising a social media dashboard.

Once you start using social networks the sheer volume of information that can start being directed at you can be a little daunting, knowing how to manage it all can be more daunting still. Previously, this was a slow and laborious task of dealing with one network at a time and one message at a time. Recently, a range of online tools has sought to make this process simpler by combining and allowing you to maintain several communications outlets at once.

When selecting a dashboard for your use, you should consider such items as cost, analytic ability and which social networks they support. These are some of my favourite for your consideration:-

### 1. HootSuite
http://hootsuite.com)
My personal favourite and the one that I use is HootSuite. You can update multiple social media platforms (including Twitter, Facebook and more) from your computer or smartphone. You can track your interactions and Hootsuite allows you to set up access for several users if you work in a team format.

There are free and paid for versions of HootSuite and it's

worth investigating which gives you the tools you need to make the most of the networks.

**2.TweetDeck**

(https://about.twitter.com/products/tweetdeck)

TweetDeck allows you to manage multiple Twitter accounts plus Facebook updates from the same dashboard. You can set up keyword searches and schedule Tweets in advance.

**3. Sprout Social**

(www.sproutsocial.com)

One of the new kids on the block, SpoutSocial supports Twitter, Facebook, Google+, LinkedIn and others. It offers a range of analytical tools but it comes at a cost. Compared to other dashboards Sprout Social is not cheap, but I have colleagues who use it and love it so it depends on your needs.

**How influential are you?**

Your web analytics will give you a good idea of which social networks are driving traffic to your website, but you might also consider your sphere of influence when it comes to social networks.

There's a great little website and app called Klout (http://klout.com). You can go to the website, connect with the social networks you use and get a Klout score. It's a nifty little measuring device that will tell you just how many people are listening to what you say. My Klout score at the moment is about 60/100. It something that I'm working on improving.

Spend some time working on Klout. As you grown more and more influential certain companies will offer you benefits including free products if you talk about their products. It's worth investigating.

# 11. SOME KEY THINGS TO CONSIDER WITH SOCIAL NETWORKS

For all you newbies to social networks and even to the rest of you who've been online for a while, consider the following principles when it comes to using networks:-

### 1. Post Often
At least once a day to maintain interest on each network you are involved in. Try to keep the posts interesting – this is not an instruction to post sales messages each day!

### 2. Post pictures
Social media is a highly visual form of communication. Use photos and videos wherever possible.

### 3. Pass It On
Don't just worry about posting your own content. Share other peoples posts as well as your own. Remember this is a network and the whole structure relies on people sharing. Share posts that you think will benefit others. It will encourage other people to share your posts.

### 4. Be Sociable
Remember, it's called 'Social Media" for a reason. Be polite, reply to a few people and post comments where possible to encourage more interaction.

# 12. CONCEPTS TO USE WITH SOCIAL NETWORKS – PART ONE

The possibilities with social networks are as endless as your imagination but here are a few thoughts that you might like to implement and experiment with.

### Involve your audience

In a recent TED (www.ted.com) discussion on Broadway, given by Randi Zuckerberg, sister of Facebook founder Mark Zuckerberg, it was suggested that social media could play an increasing role in marketing theatre by engaging audiences as never before.

Randi suggested that taking a photo of the audience at a given performance and posting it on Facebook, could get audiences reacting by tagging themselves in the photo. So what I hear you say, but think about it this way. For each person going to your Facebook page you may well end up with a new Like, you might also get seen by all of the friends of the person tagging themselves bringing awareness to your group.

*Rock Of Ages*, during its run in London posted several pictures of the audience on several nights. After the show, the audience were advised using little slips of paper that the photo could be found on Facebook with an invitation to tag themselves and add a comment. Comments like "I want to come back again badly!" and "What an amazing night!" were indicative of the comments posted. Thousands of people saw those posts. Given the first hand comments of people that they knew praising the show do you think they were more or less likely to buy a ticket?

Or try it in reverse. A big trend in the USA at the moment is to ask your audience to take a photo or the curtain call and Tweet or Facebook it as they leave the theatre with their comments.

Please note right now that I am NOT suggesting allowing photographs to be taken during a performance. I can think of nothing worse. BUT after the show has concluded, take a moment out of your curtain call to ask people to take a picture and spread it via social networking.

For most amateur groups a short run is a real obstacle, so imagine 300+ people taking a picture on your first performance and spreading it via Facebook or Twitter just to name two, to everyone they know with a great comment or mini review. Forget about waiting for radio or newspaper reviews, 300 people could instantly tell thousands that your show was great. If you are then selling tickets online, there's a strong possibility you could have sold a significant number of tickets by morning without lifting a finger. Your audience will have done the work for you.

# 13. FACEBOOK

## Who Should Use It

The Big Daddy of the social networks, Facebook is possibly the most widely used general-purpose social network that exists. Whether your desired use is personal or for your business, the chances are that Facebook is for you. Facebook is a network that now spans the globe and the chances of finding people who are not on the Facebook network becomes rarer and rarer as time goes on.

With Facebook you can share personal information, photos, significant events, videos, links to websites, play games, invite friends to join you at events, or just wish a friend Happy Birthday.

## About Facebook

Many of you will have seen the film *The Social Network* and will have a basic grasp of the story of Mark Zuckerberg and the online revolution unleashed with his website Facebook. This addictive network changed the way many of us communicate world-wide.

Facebook is also a multi-level marketing and communications tool. Most amateur theatre groups approaching the website should open their minds and investigate just how the site could work for them not only in developing and finding an audience, but also in helping to communicate with the members of the company and allowing past members to keep in touch. Many groups fail to see the possibilities and I hope that the following chapters will prove informative and eye-opening.

There's no denying that there are a LOT of people on Facebook. Do a quick search and you will most likely find the person you are looking for. Search for the name of a show, composer or playwright and you may well find several "pages" devoted to them.

The global reach of Facebook is enormous, the local reach is sizeable and your success or failure with Facebook will depend on your tapping into your local community and becoming an active part of that and other networks.

So here goes…

## The Types Of Facebook Page

I'm taking the wholesale assumption here that EVERY reader has their own Facebook account. If not put down the book and go and set one up. Not an account for your group but one for your personally. The process is simple and Facebook will guide you through it. Once you are done come back and resume reading.

Many groups are under the misapprehension that by simply setting up a Facebook group that they are on the social networking fast track. In truth, to make the most of Facebook, societies need to be looking at the platform on several different levels to properly promote their group and improve communications with their members.

As many of you know, one of the most significant features of Facebook Groups and Pages is the ability to publish stories to members and fans' news feeds. Whilst stories will not be visible to all users, Facebook wall stories can obtain a significant reach.

So here's a guide to how a group might ideally tackle Facebook to their betterment.

### The Facebook Group

If you haven't encountered Facebook Groups, there's a good chance you haven't spent more than an hour on Facebook. Facebook explains that groups are "for members of groups to connect, share and even collaborate on a given topic or idea". A Facebook Group is one where you are asked to JOIN.

The **Closed Group** represents the best network imaginable for cast and crew communications. By setting up a closed group you can invite people to join and communicate important information without the rest of the world having access. In terms of group activities this is great for arranging rehearsals, fittings, tech schedules. Most of this information is not of interest to the general public and should certainly not form part of your normal Facebook Page.

You can choose to have a closed group for the society or theatre company or one for each show produced (which is possible) but it could get a bit cumbersome if lots of shows are produced over time.

You can also choose to make your Facebook group **Secret.** This is a great way to have your group visible only to invited members. This is a great way to share production information with cast and crew without it being seen by everyone. Let's face it how interesting is rehearsal scheduling or cast social events to the outside world.

One of the best features of groups is the ability to send messages direct to members' Facebook inboxes. Messages though are restricted once a group surpasses 5,000 members. If you are looking to build a group for marketing purposes, this feature will quickly become useless as the group surpasses a certain level.

**The Facebook Page**
You see Facebook pages everyday. They are the pages that ask you to LIKE them. In contrast to groups, Facebook Pages "allow entries such as public figures and organisations to broadcast information to their fans." If you are looking to set up your company's "official Facebook presence" you should opt for Facebook Pages.

When somebody 'likes' a page, the updates from that page are included in their news feed – and that the fact that they have liked your page may show up in the news feeds of their friends. Facebook users can like individual pieces of content from pages. When someone likes or comments on a page post, that activity may also be shared with their friends, increasing your page's reach. In fact, about 30% of the content from news feeds is from pages rather than from individual profiles. This is how your group will use Facebook to promote your business: by creating a page. Encouraging people to 'like' it – and then keeping engaged with content that will appear in their news feeds.

Whilst both Groups and Pages are indexed by search engines, Facebook Pages provide administrators with greater search engine optimisation. In addition to being able to publish to fan's walls or timelines, Facebook Pages also have the ability to target stream posts based on location and language. If you have successfully attracted fans from around the world, you may wish to distribute your English content directly to English speaking fans.

Want to convert visitors to your company website into fans of your Facebook Page? Facebook provides all administrators with Facebook Fanbox widgets to help promote their Facebook pages. Facebook Groups on the other hand, have no similar feature.

### How it affects others
Organisations like Amateur Stage thrive on the ability to like your Facebook pages from their Amateur Stage Facebook Page just as regional newspapers can like your Facebook page from their Facebook Pages. Unfortunately organisations who have Pages are unable to join Groups. When Amateur Stage publish their Break a Leg messages or any other messages on our Facebook page about specific groups, they like to link to you on Facebook and whilst they can do that with Facebook Pages, they can't with Groups.

### What you need to do.

**Step one** is to establish a Page for your group.

### Creating a Facebook Page

I'm assuming that you already have an individual profile on Facebook. If not set one up for yourself. It will help you see and interact with other people as well as giving you the Launchpad to start promoting your group or project.

**To start** setting up your page go to www.facebook.com/
pages/create.php

The first step is to choose a category. There are six main
categories each with sub-categories, so think carefully
which one best reflects your business. You can change
these later by editing your page. Give you page a name –
usually your business name, but think about which search
terms people will use on Facebook to find you. Get started
and start customising.

**Like** personal profiles, your page needs a profile picture
(this can be your logo). With the timeline layout it is also
important to include a large headers image on your page
(851 x 315 pixels). Your header image may also appear on
the news feed of individuals whenever a friend of theirs
like your page – so make it eye-catching and something
that communicates your brand. Don't include marketing
text such as pricing or calls to action here though, as this
is prohibited.

**Click Show** or **Hide** at the top right of your page to reveal
or hide your **Admin Panel.** From this administrative area
you can access detailed metrics for your page, see who has
recently liked your page and which items of content are
most popular. At the top of your page are drop-down menus
called **Edit Page** and **Build Audience.** From the Edit Page
menu you can edit your page, add other administrators
and, importantly, change your 'voice' from your personal
profile name to your page name. The drop-down option
will switch (in my case) Use Facebook as PackedRaftersPr
and Use Facebook as Douglas Mayo.

**Engage people with updates.**

Now that you have a page, you need some content. The way to add this is via status updates – just as you would with your personal profile. You can pay to promote your updates – but you won't need to if you keep your content relevant to your audience, consistent and engaging enough for them to want to like, comment or share.

Content can be status updates, links, images, videos, offers, events or questions. It's a great idea to ask questions to encourage discussion. For instance - you can post a link to an opinion piece about a topic relevant to amateur theatre or your group.

Use images where possible and appropriate, since the timeline layout gives weight to these. They take up more space in news feeds, so they are seen more easily, and people are much more likely to engage with an image rather than a text-based update. To see an example of a page where images are well used check out the Facebook page for Amateur Stage Magazine (https://www.facebook.com/amateurstagemagazine).

By hovering over an individual post and clicking the down arrow to reveal a menu you can also:

• Highlight it (star icon) This makes it the full width of your page.
• Hide it or delete it.
• Change its date (clock icon)
• Pin it (choose Pin To Top). This anchors your post to the top of your page for up to seven days, meaning it won't disappear down your timeline as your new post updates.

## Promote Your Page

The most important thing now is to promote your page. Blog about it, tweet about it and include it in your email signature. Ask all the members of your group to like your page and mention it to all of their Facebook friends.

The most important page to do this is on your blog or website, by enabling people to 'like' your page directly without even having to visit Facebook. You may need to get some help with this if you are not a knowledgeable website person but your webmaster should be able to do this for you.

Create your Facebook 'like' box at http://developers. facebook.com/docs/reference/plugins/like-box. You can create a 'like' box for any Facebook page from here – just enter the URL for your page, and start customising. The most minimal option is simply to display your page's profile image, name and a 'like' button. Then simply add the code provided to your website.

## Measure your results

With Facebook groups, you have very little more than the number of members to go on, but with pages, facebook matrics really come into their own, and this is a key reason for using pages in the first place.

The most obvious measure of your success is your number of fans. Fans are important because they have potential to see your updates in their news feed, but this is a fairly blunt measure. A more important measure is the level of engagement fans have with your page. Engagement here is defined as clicking anywhere in a post, including liking, commenting and sharing your content.

To access your stats, click **Show** at the top right of your page to reveal your **Admin Panel**. Click **See All** next to the Insights graph towards the bottom. The summary figures at the top show:

- **Total Likes** – how many people like your page.
- **Friends of fans** – the number of fans plus all their friends
- **People talking about this** – the number of people who have 'created a story' about your page. In Facebook terms, this means people who have liked, posted or shared your page or page content.
- **Weekly total reach** – people who have seen any content associated with your page.

Below the graph, there are detailed insights for every page post, which relate to the first 28 days after posting. You can click on the numbers given for the first three metrics for further breakdown:

- **Reach** – the number of unique people who saw your post
- **Engaged users** – how many clicked on your post
- **Talking about this** – the number of likes, comments and shares
- **Virality** – the percentage of unique people who saw your post who created a story about it.

These metrics are all available on the **Overview** page view, which is selected by default. There are additional links next to this at the top of your **Insights** page: Likes, Reach and Talking About This, all if which give you detailed demographic information about your fans. Likes is the most useful here. The information about your fans can be useful for market research, developing new products or services or just gaining a better understanding of you're your customers are. It includes demographic breakdown by age, gender, geographic location and language.

Aside from your Insights page, you can also see how many people saw a particular post by looking at the link underneath it, which will say something like '542 people saw this post'. Hovering over this will break it down by organic and viral; and show you a link to stats for your most popular post, which can act as a benchmark of what you can achieve. Use these metrics to assess which types of post work best with your audience.

## FACEBOOK PAGES ARE NOT A REPLACEMENT FOR A WEBSITE

Yes, Facebook pages are free to set up but they are in no way a replacement for an updated website. At the present time it is against Facebook rules to point your domain name at a Facebook page, so don't even go there. Social networks are a well presented business card for your group and should be used as such. A good Facebook or Twitter campaign will drive people to your website.

# 14. CONCEPTS TO USE WITH SOCIAL NETWORKING – PART TWO

"Tagging" is one of the features that Facebook gives to users and it's amazing just how many people are ignorant to its uses or only utilise a part of what's on offer.

**So what is tagging and how does it work?**
A tag is a special kind of link. When you tag someone, you create a link to their Timeline. The post you tag the person in may also be added to that person's Timeline. For example, you can tag a photo to show who's in the photo or post a status update and say who you're with. If you tag a friend in your status update, anyone who sees that update can click on your friend's name and go to their Timeline. Your status update may also show up on that friend's Timeline.

When you tag someone, they'll be notified. Also, if you or a friend tags someone in your post and the post is set to Friends or more, the post could be visible to the audience you selected plus friends of the tagged person.

You can also tag people in status updates and other posts from yourself. It's another way to let people know who and what you are talking about.

People often update their status to reflect their thoughts and feelings, or to mention things they feel like sharing. Sometimes that includes referencing friends, groups or even events they are attending — for instance, posting "Grabbing lunch with Meredith Chin" or "I'm heading to Starbucks Coffee Company — anyone want some coffee?".

When you are writing a status update and want to add a friend's name to something you are posting, just include the "@" symbol beforehand. As you type the name of what you would like to reference, a drop-down menu will appear that allows you to choose from your list of friends and other connections, including groups, events, applications and Pages. Soon, you'll be able to tag friends from applications as well. The "@" symbol will not be displayed in the published status update or post after you've added your tags.

Friends you tag in your status updates will receive a notification and a Wall post linking them to your post. They also will have the option to remove tags of themselves from your posts. We hope that tagging your status updates and others posts from the Publisher will enable you to share in a more meaningful and engaging way, and connect with even more people. We're rolling this feature out over the course of the next few weeks, so you may not see the new feature just yet.

You will usually need to Like the person you are tagging or to Like As Your Page before Facebook will give you the ability to include people in a tag but this is a simple process and in the long run it will improve your audience.

# 15. TWITTER

## What is Twitter?

Since its creation in 2006 by Jack Dorsey, Biz Stone, Noah Glass and Evan Williams, Twitter has gained international popularity as a social network with over 500 million users sending over 340 million tweets per day.

According to HubSpot, 42% of companies have acquired a customer via Twitter.

The concept is simple. Twitter encourages you to record your thoughts or send a message in 'tweets' – each 'tweet' being an update of 140 or fewer characters. Keep it simple and concise is very much the essence of what Twitter is about.

You can use Twitter to communicate with people, companies, theatre groups that you know, or find new people or groups who interest you, or both.

Twitter works on the premise that everything that happens on the network is in response to the basic question 'What are you doing?' By going to www.twitter.com you can have an account established and be tweeting to the world in a relatively short time.

**Things to consider**

**Step One – Signing Up or Registration**

Go to www.twitter.com and fill in your FULL NAME, EMAIL ADDRESS and nominate your PASSWORD

The site will then ask you to confirm your details and ask you to choose a USERNAME. Once you have completed this screen Twitter will guide you through the set up process in a simple fashion designed to get you Tweeting as quickly as possible. Think carefully about your Twitter username. Make it functional and easy to remember

You immediately have an opportunity to FOLLOW people you like. Type in the name of your theatre group, Amateur Stage, Samuel French, Josef Weinberger or Theatrical Rights and join those people or organisations that are of interest to your group.

Don't forget to follow us @packedrafterspr for more great marketing and pr tips after you've finished reading this book.

You're also able to import your email contacts into Twitter. Twitter will search your contacts and identify your friends on Twitter using their email addresses. I'd suggest going back to this function at a later time particularly if you are setting up an account for your group. There may be people in your email contacts who you don't want linked to your amateur theatre group so don't rush into this function, you can come back to it.

If at anytime you want to skip a step in Twitter's suggested set up process just hit the Skip button on the left hand side of the screen.

After these steps you'll be asked to upload a profile picture. This can be your groups logo or perhaps you'd prefer to use a pic from a recent production. The choice is yours. You can also fill in a brief bio. You have 160 characters to say something brief about you.

That's it – you should now have a Twitter account. Twitter will send you an email to confirm your email address. You'll see a prompt at the top of the screen advising you to CHECK YOUR EMAIL.

Once your confirmed you'll be diving into Twitter at the deep end and the fun begins.

There are four main views available once you have signed in. The navigation links at the top left of your screen are:

• **Home** – the latest tweets for everyone you follow.

• **Connect** – your 'Interactions' – i.e. whenever anyone includes your @username, retweets or favourites your tweet, follows you or adds you to a list, this action will show up here.

• **Discover** – a little more like Facebook news feed, this shows a timeline of recent tweets tailored to what Twitter thinks you will be interested in.

• **Me** – your profile page, showing your biography and the latest tweets you have posted. This is what people see when they visit your Twitter account. This also displays a count of how many tweets they have posted, how many people you follow and how many followers you have.

Next to this is a search box, and a cog wheel icon, which includes the drop down menu options Edit profile, Direct Messages, Lists and Settings. Direct messages (DM) are private messages and can be sent to anyone who follows you. Lists are useful for creating a discrete list of people on Twitter whose tweets you want to view in a separate timeline. You can also sign out of your account from here, and sign into another account. Finally, at the right-hand side of the top bar is a blue button with a quill pen icon. Click this to write a new tweet. There are two icons below your text window: a camera (to upload an image) and a map pin (to add your location).

Other links below a tweet may include 'View conversation', 'View summary', 'View photo', or 'View video'. But it's the links that only become visible when you hiver over a tweet that you will use the most:

• **Reply** – send a reply that starts with @username. This is visible to anyone who visits your profile and in the timelines of anyone who follows both you and the person you are replying to. Mentions, by contrast, are used to mean a mention of someone's @username within a tweet and are more visible.

• **Retweet** – pass a tweet on to your followers. Visible on your profile page and in the timelines of people who follow you. Displays the profile picture and the name of the original tweeter with 'Retweeted by [Your Name]' underneath. You can also 'manually' retweet by tweeting 'RT@username:' followed by a cut-and-pasted tweet.

• **Favourite** – add a tweet to your list of favourites. Other people can see these by clicking 'Favourites' on your profile. This can be a useful place to save any client testimonials or positive customer feedback.

• **More** – used less often, but it can be useful to 'Email Tweet' to someone or 'Embed Tweet' on your blog or website with the code provided.

Also, on the left-hand sidebar you will find:

• **Media** – on your profile page only, a collection of thumbnail images of images you have uploaded and videos you have shared.

• **Who To Follow** – suggestions based on the people you follow already – and who they follow.

• **Trending topics** – the 10 most commonly-used words or phrases being used on Twitter right now. These may or not be hashtags, and can be viewed as global trends or narrowed down geographically.

**A few pointers.**

1. Don't be afraid to show some personality in your tweets. 87% of users said they followed brands for 'fun and entertainment'. Keep it informal, and personable but relevant.

2. About half the people who use Twitter use it from their phones making it a great way to get out last minute and current information.

3. According to a 2011 survey by Compete, 94% of Twitter users follow brands for 'discounts and promos', and 88% for 'free stuff'. It's worth keeping this in mind if you are planning any ticketing offers.

## What are Hastags?

Hashtags (#) are simply clickable keywords. Put the # symbol immediately before a word or phrase (with no spaces or punctuation) and it becomes a link. When someone clicks on a hashtag, it will link through to a new timeline made up of everyone who has included that hashtag in their tweets. Hashtags are often used to discuss and follow an event in real time.

## Keep it brief.

Tweets are most useful when they include a relevant link to something useful or interesting. Although Twitter will shorten links for you, to make the most out of your 140 characters, the URL shortening service Bitly (http://bitly. com) is most useful because you can use it on multiple Twitter accounts and it comes with metrics on click-throughs.

## Building your followers.

Building followers on Twitter is akin to building an email list. In the world of social media these people are valued because they have chosen to follow you because they are interested in what you have to say. Once your list builds you can make production announcements, advise of auditions or anything else that is of interest to your followers, but as with all social media try to avoid doing the hard sell wherever possible.

The big secret is simply: follow more people. At least half will follow you back but please bear in mind:

1. Only follow people who are in your interest group. Follow people who are likely to be interested in you and follow you back. Use the hashtag to find people like yourself, who are tweeting in your subject area. I've found that many people in amateur theatre use #amdram. You can also look at the Twitter directory WeFollow (http://wefollow.com).

2. Stay within the follow limit. There is a limit – you can't just follow everyone. Twitter will stop you from following new people once you hit the limit. However, the limit increases the more followers you have. You can follow 2,000 people, but after that you can follow roughly 10% more people than are following you.

3. Unfollow people, who don't follow you back. Don't be afraid to unfollow people from your Twitter account. You don't want disinterested people clogging up your Twitter account so by clearing them out you make space for you to follow new people. You can find those people who you follow but who don't follow you by using Friend or Follow (http://friendorfollow.com)

Yes, it's a bit time consuming, but by following this strategy you can increase your followers to high levels in a relatively short space of time. Once you reach a critical mass of followers, your Twitter success will build on itself.

**Keep it short!**
With only 140 characters, there's no surprise that abbreviations abound on Twitter. Here is a major one that will be important to you.

**RT = Retweet.**
A quick way of asking anyone who sees you post to send it out to their followers.

# 16. CONCEPTS TO USE WITH SOCIAL NETWORKING - PART THREE

**Follow Friday** is a unique phenomenon on Twitter that is really catching on.

**Follow Friday** or **#ff** on Twitter is a tradition in which people send tweets recommending Twitter users they think other people may be interested in following.

The tweets are sent on Fridays and contain the hashtag (keyword preceded by the pound symbol) #ff or #FollowFriday.

The idea is to help people figure out who to follow on Twitter by sharing usernames or Twitter handles of your favorite Twitterers, the people whose tweets you find interesting. It's all about helping people get followers on Twitter.

Follow Friday is an informal, loosely organized system that requires no registration or special formatting in order to participate. Some even consider it a game--it's mainly for fun. People do it to be good doobies and praise the people they admire.

### History of Follow Friday or #FF on Twitter
The Follow Friday tradition started when a Twitter user named Micah Baldwin thought it would be a good idea for everyone to suggest people to follow in tweets. He decided to make it happen on Fridays and give it that name, Follow Friday. Another user suggested adding the #followfriday

hashtag, which other people later shortened to #ff.

The Friday endorsements caught on quickly, and now a variety of sites exist to help promote them.

FollowFriday.com, for example, tracks who's being recommended and who's doing the recommendations.

FollowFridayHelper (www.followfridayhelper.com) is a special app that tracks who you interact with the most on Twitter. It offers shortcuts to promote them and express gratitude to those who recommend you on Twitter.

**How to Participate in Follow Friday**
First, decide who you want to recommend. It's common to recommend several people at once.

Be sure you write down their Twitter user names carefully and double-check your spelling.

Now create a new tweet that starts with your list of user names to be recommended. Put the @ symbol before each Twitter user name and separate the names with a space or comma. At the end of your tweet, insert the #ff hashtag.

A typical Follow Friday tweet might be a simple list of user names and look like this: @amateurstage @packedrafterspr @amdramcouk #ff

If you have room, it's also a good idea to include a thought about why other people should follow the folks you are recommending. That works best when you are only recommending one user, or have a common reason for recommending several. The more guidance or specificity you offer, the greater the likelihood that other people will check out your suggestions.

### What is the Future for Follow Friday?

As Twitter has grown exponentially, the sense of fellowship and community around #FF tweets has grown harder to maintain.

Its utility does not seem to be as strong as it once was, especially as more commercial use and marketing have mushroomed on Twitter and infiltrated the Follow Friday tweets.

Yet all in all, Twitter's #Follow Friday tradition remains popular. It's an international messaging system, so it's not surprising that the end-of-week recommendation tradition has become popular around the world.

### Six Ways to Increase Your Twitter Followers:

### 1. Start following other people.

Find people with interests similar to yours and follow them. That, in turn, will help you get Twitter followers. This is the most basic and quick way to build get followers on Twitter who will really add value to your Twitter experience.

As you start following people, you'll find a snowball will slowly start rolling. The people you choose to follow will often check you out on Twitter as soon as they see you are following them. If they like what they see, they may click the "follow" button, too, and become one of your followers. When that happens, other people will soon see you on Twitter, too.

## A Good Profile Helps Get Followers

Be sure to complete your Twitter profile first, before you do much following or tweeting. Invest time in learning the basics of how to use Twitter. Too many novices make the mistake of charging blindly ahead with no clue of how Twitter works.

Before you start following people, it's important to be ready for people to check you out. Complete your profile and have interesting tweets in your timeline before you start following the people you really want to follow you back. Otherwise, if you have not tweeted yet or filled out your profile, these folks likely will click away without electing to follow you.

Make sure that at a minimum, you have a photo of yourself on your profile page and have written a few words about yourself or your business in the bio area. Clearly identify yourself, too. People rarely follow mysterious, cute, or clever names without knowing who's behind that Twitter handle.

Another reason you should start following people is that the more people who follow you, the more likely their followers are to check you out as a follower of someone they follow. This is the snowball effect--you start following people and some of them will follow you. Then some of their followers will check you out, too.

## 2. Be sure to follow those who follow you, or at least many of them.

If you don't follow people who have taken the trouble to follow you, some of them may get irked and unfollow you. In addition to being good Twitter etiquette, following your followers may cause them to engage with you publicly on their timelines, attracting more attention from their followers. Again, it's the snowball effect.

### 3. Tweet Regularly to Get Twitter Followers

Tweeting at least once a day will help you get Twitter followers. Updating frequently (but not TOO frequently) also will make more people want to follow you.

What is the right frequency for tweeting? Ideally, at least once or twice a day, but no more than half a dozen in one day. And if you do tweet frequently, use a Twitter tool to time your tweets and space them out; don't send a barrage all at once.

### 4. Tweet about interesting topics and use popular hashtags.

The more you tweet about topics and hashtags that other people are interested in, the more likely they are to see your tweets when they run searches on those keywords and hashtags. If they like a tweet you send, they may click on your Twitter handle to check you out.

Tweeting high quality content about topics relevant to your followers' interests truly is the best way to build and retain a large following on Twitter in the long run. It take time to build a following this way, but your ability to retain followers will be greater than if you try to get followers on Twitter quickly using many of the automatic follower strategies.

### 5. Thou shall not spam. Ever.

A word about how NOT to get followers on Twitter: The quickest way to lose followers is to use your tweets to advertise or try to sell products or services. People are on Twitter to converse and learn. Twitter is not TV!

**6. Consider more than just numbers on Twitter.**
This is also known as the quality vs. quantity debate.

So far, we've mostly talked about the numbers game, how to get followers of any kind. But if you are using Twitter to promote your career or business, you should be careful to get Twitter followers who will be appropriate for your goals. That means choosing a Twitter strategy and targeting followers thoughtfully, rather than taking a scattershot approach.

Much debate occurs over whether people should pursue quantity or quality as they try to get Twitter followers. Would you rather have more followers of any kind, or fewer followers who are interested in the same things you are? Most experts advocate quality over quantity, though both have their role in any strategy for using Twitter in marketing.

If you do care about quality at all, you should go out of your way to avoid tactics for getting Twitter followers that might backfire by alienating the people you really want to keep and causing them to unfollow you. Many auto follow methods fall into this category.

And if you're using Twitter for business, most social media experts will tell you that it simply doesn't pay to overdo it on following people or getting too many followers. In the long run, it can reduce the actual value you get from Twitter by cluttering your Twitter stream with messages from people whose interests don't overlap with yours.

## 17. GOOGLE +

**What is Google +**
Launched in 2011, Google+ is the latest social network from Google. Google has attempted forays into the social networking sphere before without much success so in its early days many where sceptical about spending time on Google+ but unlike its predecessors it's still running and it now seems to be building some momentum so it's worth considering as one of your social media platforms.

Google+ can look a little confusing at first but at it's core it operates in similar ways to Facebook but it just uses different terminology. Instead of friending or following people, you add them to circles. Posts to the site are usually called stories. Instead of liking you show your appreciation with a +1 and if you like a story you can reshare it.

The main features of Google+ are displayed down the left-hand side of your page in a vertical navigation bar, though you need to hover over the item shown (initially 'Home') to see the full menu:

• **Home** – equivalent to the newsfeed on Facebook. You can filter what you see in your stream by circles once you have some set up – just click the name of the circle you'd like to see stories from. Your right-hand sidebar shows a list of people in your circles who have enabled video chat with you (known as hangouts).

• **Profile** – your profile page is what people see when they visit your page. The default view is Posts – stories that you have posted and shared – but people can also view your

About page. Other tabs that may or may not be visible to visitors depending on your settings are Photos, You Tube, your +1s and reviews.

• **People** – find people to add to your circles, see who has added you to their circles and manage your own circles.

• **Photos** – upload, back up and organise your photos.

• **What's hot** – content that is recommended from across Google+

• **Communities** – on Google + communities are a bit like groups on Facebook. Depending on the settings of the community you want to join, you can either join it instantly and start contributing, or ask to join.

• **Events** – integrated with Google Calendar. Events are a way of inviting people to and managing events on Google+. Everyone at an event can contrinute their photos directly to one shared photo collection. There's even a party mode where people can snap photos in real time from the event, from their phones.

• **Hangouts on Air** – a feature that makes Google+ stand out from other social networks is video chat, or hangouts. Start a hangout with up to nine friends, accept hangout invitations from others or chat one-to-one. You can do this from your right-hand sidebar. Hangouts on Air are hangouts that people have made public. These are also recorded and saved for later viewing.

• **Pages** – create and manage your business page from here.

• **Local** – people can 'check-in', review locations and add photos, With Google+ Local, all their reviews and associated photos are visible to everyone on the web, under your name.

• **Settings** – manage your account, security, profile and privacy settings from here.

### Search Engine Benefits
There is one over-ridding benefit of having a Google+ account – even if you never use it- and that is the search engine benefit. Google+ is owned by Google, the largest and most popular search engine in the world, with that being the case which page do you think will appear first if someone Googles your name or business name? Google+ helps Google to improve its search engine results through the information it is able to collect from your social circle.

### What are circles?
On Facebook you send friend requests, on Twitter you follow people but on Google+ you add people to circles.

It's a powerful concept that solves problems and helps you market your theatre group.

With Google+ you can share posts with who you want to. You can mark updates public, or just share them with specific circles or even individuals. This helps you to filter your message to the right people – but also helps you to keep your content relevant.

However, just because you have added someone to your circles doesn't mean they will necessarily see anything you post; that will only happen if someone adds you to their circles. When you add someone, their public posts appear in your home stream and the streams of any circles you have added them to. The posts they share with specific circles are only visible to you if you are in one of those circles. You therefore, need more people to add you to their circles in order for Google+ to become a useful marketing tool.

### Creating Circles

You can create new circles whenever you add someone, which you can do from their Google+ page. There are essentially two ways to categorise people into circles:

• **Relationship Circles** might include 'Family', 'Friends' and 'Clients' – use these to manage your professional relationships, and to keep your personal and business lives separate if you wish.

• **Interest circles** might include 'Theatre', 'Musicals' or 'Plays' – use these to segment your marketing messages to the most receptive audience and keep your content relevant.

You can create as many circles as you want and call them what you like – experiment and see what works for you.

### Start Sharing

Once you have your circles set up, you can share posts or 'stories' with people in them. You can make your posts visible to:

• **Public** – anyone on the internet, including those searching Google, so it's a good idea to make most of your posts public.

• **Your circles** – anyone who is in at least one of your circles.

• **Extended Circles** – your circles plus people in their circles.

• **A community** – if you choose to share with a community, you can only share with that community and not Public or Circles as well.

### Create a Community
Pages are useful for building a following around your group or show. Communities help build brand loyalty, and position you as knowledgeable in a certain field. They are most effective if they focus on discussion around topics related to your business. Communities on Google+ are the equivalent to groups on Facebook or LinkedIn, and are a powerful way to reach a lot of people at once. There are two main ways to use them: join some communities, and start your own.

### Join some communities
Go to the Communities tab and see suggestions and search for communities to join in your topic area. Try searching for amateur theatre, amdram, musical theatre or plays. Communities may be public or private – i.e. joined instantly by anyone, or subject to approval of requests to join. Join some that are relevant to your interests and/or business.

### Start your own community
Once you have become familiar with how communities work by joining a few, it is time to have a go at creating one of your own. If you start your own community, you can begin building your own list of members. To get started, just go to the communities tab and click on the Create community button.

**A few things to consider.**

I would general recommend making your community public to make it more visible and to attract more members. Add your About text. Tell people who your community is for and describe it in an interesting way. Set guidelines advising how you would like people within your community to behave. I suggest moderating posts to maintain their value. You can easily add more moderators to your community to help you maintain the content within it. You can easily use Categories to organise discussions and once you have some content up and running invite people to join in.

# 18. CONCEPTS TO USE WITH SOCIAL NETWORKING – PART 4

Many people ask me just "How much is to much when it comes to social networking?" Can you post too many times?

There is no definitive answer to this question. The tolerance to how much content you place 'out there' via social networks is very much determined by the tolerance of your audience, and the only way to find this out is via experimentation.

For example, a while ago on the Amateur Stage Facebook page, we used to post a series of 'Break A Leg' messages. Each message contained a show poster or image and a message to specific groups wishing them good luck for their forthcoming seasons. Each message would link to the groups respective Facebook fan pages (wherever possible) and if possible link to their website or online box office.

Given that there are thousands of groups in the UK, you can imagine the number of messages that went out at times, especially on popular production weeks. With just over 1000 Facebook fans at that stage, one morning we got a quite eloquent complaint from a Facebook fan, who, said we were filling his wall with what he called junk and would we please stop.

I decided the best thing to do was to pose the question to the group via the Facebook wall. We asked if others thought there were too many posts going up. Hundreds of responses later we got an overwhelming 100% response from our Followers that they liked what we were doing, and this one complaint was not representative of the masses. Needless to say we continued.

What I am saying is that your followers and audience will quickly tell you if you are going overboard. Just remember though, that posting for the sheer sake of it won't do you any good. You need to have something to say and make the quality of your posts the most important factor in when and how often you post.

# 19. PINTEREST

One of the fastest growing social networks is one based purely on images. Pinterest was launched in 2010 and by 2013 had over 70 million users.

In basic terms Pinterest is a form of virtual noticeboard. It's a place to 'pin' your interests. You can create notice boards based on various topics and then pin your images to them. You can upload these images, but most are usually pinned from websites using a 'pin it' button on your browser toolbar, and link back to them. You can add your own descriptions, and other people can like and comment on your pins, and 'repin' or share them on their own boards. Just like Twitter, people can follow people on Pinterest and they can follow you. With Pinterest though, you are allowed to be a bit more selective by either following all of someone's boards, or just those that interest you the most.

The main navigation options are in a bar across the top of your page:
• **Pinterest** – the Pinterest logo in the centre of the bar is also your link to your 'Home Feed' default view. This shows the latest pins from everyone you follow, plus your latest notifications of anyone who has commented, liked or repined one of your pins.

• **Browse** – clicking on the square icon with the three horizontal lines at the left of the screen opens a list of about three dozen categories from architecture to tattoos. Useful for browsing pins by category.

• **Search** – enter a keyword into the search box, and then filter your results by Boards, Pins or Pinners. This is a useful way of finding boards to follow, pins to repin and pinners to follow.

Click the + button to create a board or manually upload an image and specify which web address you want it to link to. You can also add a pin from a website here, though normally you will use the 'Pin It' button for this.

Click your account name on the right hand side to reveal the following drop-down options:

• **Your boards** – this links to your profile, which is what others see when they visit your Pinterest URL e.g. www. pinterest.com/amateurstage. You can also see a couple of things tat casual visitors can't: 1. A 'Create a board' button at the top and 2. Up to three 'Secret Boards' at the bottom.

• **Your pins** – your latest pins displayed in reverse chronological order, regardless of which board they were pinned to.

• **Your likes** – the latest pins you have liked.

• **Settings** – modify your email notifications here, and link to your Facebook and Twitter accounts – useful for reaching a wider audience with your pins.

There is also a Help Centre, an invitation to Find Friends and a link to Log Out. Finally, click the speech bubble icon next to your name to see your latest notification.

**Why Pinterest?**

With Pinterest you can share images that encourage click-throughs to your website. This is the point of Pinterest from a marketing point of view: it's really just another social bookmarking site, since people use it to share links to other websites. According to a 2012 study, Pinterest drives more referral traffic than Google+, YouTube and LinkedIn combined. The links are also more permanent than those shared on twitter, as they are more likely to be discovered, shared and clicked on long after links shared on Twitter have disappeared way down your timeline.

Each image you pin links back to your own website. You can also upload images, and specify where they should link to. This is what drives referral traffic from Pinterest. Use automatic Tweets and Facebook shares of your pins and the effect is multiplied.

You can benefit from Pinterest even without having an account by making your own web pages pinnable. For this you need to do two things:

1. **Include images**. Include at least one image on every web page of blog post you want people to be able to pin. Make sure this is a reasonable sized one too, not just a thumbnail. If you don't have images, people can't pin your page.

2. **Encourage sharing**. Use a 'pin It' social bookmarking button – either the button provided by Pinterest or a Word Press pugin such as Shareaholic, which includes a 'Pin this' button.

**Add the 'Pin It' button to your toolbar**

Before you start pinning, you need to add the 'Pin It'

button to your browser's toolbar. You can upload images to Pinterest and enter the website you want them to link to manually. But Pinterest works best – and saves you time – when you use the 'Pin It' button.

1. Go to the Goodies page at http://about.pinterest.com/goodies.

2. Scroll down until you see the red Pin It button – and drag it to your browsers toolbar.

**Get your webmaster's help with this**
With Pinterest you can also go through the extra step of verifying your website. This involves placing some Pinterest code onto your website. This is worth doing, as it will allow you to highlight your full web address on your profile and adds a checkmark next to it here and in search results. After verification you can remove the code iof you wish.

**What sort of things can I pin?**
Once you've got the hang of boards and pinning you can start getting strategic. How will you use your boards and what will you pin to enagege your audience and drive traffic to your website?

1. **Your shows** – listing your productions is the most obvious marketing method. Try to keep separate boards for your shows.

2. **Your blog posts** – Pin every post to Pinterest – making sure each has a pinnable image, of course. If a post doesn't seem to fit, create a new board so it does. Take advantage of the referral traffic Pinterest drives to benefit your blog.

3. **Contests** - Photo contests are very popular on many social networks, and Pinterest is an obvious place for these. Invite people to submit photo entries by pinning them to their own boards with a specific hashtag in the description (so you can track entries). Repin entries to one of your own boards set up for the contest, and judge the winner, perhaps partly by number of likes or repins.

4. **Promotions** – use boards for specific themed promotions. These might be seasonal or tied to a specific production in your season.

5. **Locations** – No matter where you work in theatre, showing your workplace, rehearsal room or theatre, who works there and what they are doing can be an engaging way to give followers a 'backstage pass' to your group.

6. **Tutorials** – use Pinterest to share practical tips and information related to your group or to theatre in general. Make up tutorials, acting workshops etc can all be linked by pin toa blog post where people can find more information. Because you can also pin videos, pin any video tutorials you create too.

7. **Text** - Although images work best, it is also possible to pin text. Use Share as Image (http://shareasimage.com), which lets you highlight text anywhere on the web and turn it into an image. This is most useful for pinning famous quotations, which people tend to like and repin.

### Is Pinterest working for me?

We recommend PinReach and PinAlerts to help you keep track of your Pinterest successes.

**PinReach** (www.pinreach.com) tracks your repins and likes and to find out which pins and boards are the most popular – it also tracks click-throughs to your site.

**PinAlerts** (www.pinalerts.com) sends an email whenever someone pins something from your website.

# 20. CONCEPTS FOR USE WITH SOCIAL NETWORKING – PART 5

I referred earlier to a TED discussion by Randi Zuckerberg. Whilst the overall discussion was very much a look at social network marketing aimed at Broadway, it was a viewpoint of someone who was a tiny bit naive when it came to marketing practices.

Nevertheless, sometimes it is great to hear ideas from someone in that position. They come to the table without cluttered pre-conceived notions or ideas with limitations. I believe that whilst some of her ideas were probably not workable in the form she presented them, if modified could actually help brining audiences to theatre.

In that spirit I thought it worth listing some of her other ideas for you to digest.

So here goes:-

1. **Open auditions on You Tube** – casting a minor part with someone who has auditioned via the social media video platform.

2. **A mobile Playbill** – could you put your show programme onto a handheld device? Could it then be developed to update audiences on your next show?

3. **Crowd-sourcing** – could you appeal to your audiences to help with costumes, props or sets. This would give audiences a sense of ownership of the show.

4. **Live Tweeting** – could you have someone at the show on opening night tweeting progress reports to tell people at home how well its going?

5. **Partner with local businesses to expand audiences** – partner with local businesses to create a hashtag that can be used to promote an experience centred around your show which might include dinner etc at a local restaurant.

6. **Use photos** – a photo is worth a thousand likes!. Apart from the idea we mentioned earlier about photographing audiences for tagging, why not photograph people in the foyer and post those pictures on Facebook or Pinterest? Show people having a good time at your event and get them to go home and tag themselves.

7. **Social media walk on roles** – Literally we are talking about walking across the stage- nothing more. It's an experience few people will have and chances are you can get the person to Tweet and Facebook about their experience. Who are the influencers in your community who could go crazy with an idea like this. Use Klout to find out who has the widest sphere of influence and invite them to take part.

As I said, many of these ideas are naïve in approach, however I can see several here that I could implement with almost every amateur group I know, and in doing so get them amazing online coverage that would help them sell tickets.

Don't be closed to new ideas. They may just need some tweaking to become successful marketing tools.

# 21. LINKEDIN

With over 225 million users in 200 countries, LinkedIn is the world's largest professional social network. It may be considerably smaller than Facebook or Twitter, but it has a niche focus on professional networking that may prove useful to many.

## What is LinkedIn?

Initially LinkedIn was a place to keep your CV online and make business connections in cyberspace, but it has evolved into a more social tool. It has features such as groups and company pages, similar to the features you might use on Facebook or Google+ but they are focused to a business and professional audience. LinkedIn is worth a look even if you just set up a profile then ignore it, since it's another place for people to find you. You may well be surprised though by it's marketing potential, particularly when it comes to business to business to business (B2B) marketing. LinkedIn for me has proven to be a great place to identify potential sponsors or companies that can help us develop. Recently, LinkedIn has been slimmed down and simplified. The three main services that you will use are:

1. **Profile** – your online CV or resume – important for building trust and connections on LinkedIn. LinkedIn is an even more closed network than Facebook, and you can only send connection invitations to people you know, have some business connections with, whose email address you know, or who you have been introduced to through a mutual contact.

2. **Company pages** – Similar to business pages on Facebook or Google+, these allow you to present your brand and promote your business.

3. **Groups** – Groups are great for building a large following around a niche topic and can be a great way to engage your community with useful content and build a mailing list.

There are five main navigation links:

1. **Home** – similar to Facebook, this is your newsfeed of updates, links and activity from your network. You can also post status updates from here, which can be made visible to everyone or just shared with your connections. Updates can be liked, commented on or shared.

2. **Profile** – Your personal profile or online CV/Resume – which can also be edited from this page.

3. **Network** – the main Network link (or its Contacts sub-menu link) can be used to view and organise your network. You can also send messages to discrete segments of your network, which can be a powerful tool.

4. **Jobs** – search for jobs or post jobs (a paid for service)

5. **Interests**-click the Companies drop-down link to see the company pages you follow or manage your own. Use the Groups drop-down link to see groups you are a member of or to create a new one. You can also follow Influencers from here.

The demographic for linked in is an older one. The majority of their members are over 35 and the overage age is mid-forties. Its members are senior, affluent, influential and open for business and are usually happy to do business with you online. Don't Spam on LinkedIn or go off topic. It is a business network – so promoting your business on it is fine. Just keep it relevant to the people you are talking to.

**How LinkedIn can help you:**

### 1. Building business connections
Whether its re-establishing contact with old colleagues or meeting new contacts, LinkedIn is like a big networking event where everyone is handing out business cards. Use it to tell people what you do, but also for introductions and recommendations. In addition it is a useful way to make connections with key decision makers at organisations you want to do business with. LinkedIn will show you a number of contacts, but it will then also calculate a number of other contacts that may be of interest to you in your wider network of friends of friends. It's incredible to see which people your business contacts know in front of you on your screen and then have the luxury of deciding who you think it might be useful for you to know.

### 2. Positioning yourself as an expert
Share information about your area of expertise, whether via your profile, company page, the professional groups you are a member of, or through your own group. The core of a LinkedIn group is the discussion area, if you have knowledge to share you can position yourself as an expert.

### 3. Promoting your business
The best tools to promote your business on LinkedIn are free: company pages and groups. People can 'follow' company pages and receive your 'Company Updates', as

well as use them to learn more about your company, your products and services, and your job opportunities. Groups are useful as topic-based communities. Join groups in your area of interest, and post relevant messages to them. Then create your own to engage your community of interest with useful information, and build a new 'list' of members.

**How it works?**

There are three main steps when it comes to Linked-In

**1. Optimise your profile**
In order to use the promotional features offered by Linked-In effectively, you must have a good profile. This is the foundation of Linked-In, which is built around trusted contacts. Specifically, if you want to build a company page, one of the pre-requisites is to have a 'profile strength' that is listed as 'Intermediate' or 'All Star". That means you need a fairly complete and detailed profile.

For LinkedIn, imagine you are updating your CV or resume, focus on your career history, education, achievements and what you can offer your contacts through your business. Add links to your websites so that people can find more information, and use plenty of keywords relevant to your industry, to boost your search results. Your latest activity shows at the top of your profile – but you can drag and drop the other 'boxes' of information around, so make sure you have the most important things higher up. This will probably be your summary, but you might also want your experience, productions or projects high up too.

Build your network by importing your email contacts and searching for your business contacts. Look at your contacts' connections too for anyone you know. LinkedIn will also suggest people to connect to, based on your network, and is remarkably good at finding people for you.

One part of your profile is 'Recommendations' – short testimonials written by contacts with whom you have done business. These are equivalent to references you may include with your CV or resume, and don't be afraid to ask for them. There's even a form to make it easy for you (www. linkedin.com/recRequests).

Bear in mind that your audience in LinkedIn may be different from your audience on Facebook or Twitter. With all those social networks, keep your status updates and postings relevant to your community of interest and the networks you're communicating on.

## 2. Setting up your company page

A company page is a place where you can build a following and showcase products and services. Any LinkedIn member can follow a company that has set up a company page to get 'Company Updates'. Because you can list information about your product (or production) and provide a lot of information about each, company pages are also an opportunity for LinkedIn members to research your products and services. You can add a new company page if you meet all of the following requirements:

• You're a current company employee and your position is listed in the 'Experience' section on your profile.

• You have a company email address added and confirmed on your LinkedIn account – and your company's email domain is unique to the company (i.e. not Hotmail).

• You have several connections and you profile strength is listed as 'Intermediate' or 'All Star'.

Then select Companies from the Interests menu on the homepage and look for the name of your company. Click Edit at the top right of the Company Overview tab. If the Edit link is not visible, do the following to ensure that your profile is properly connected to the company name:

1. Click **Profile** at the top of your Homepage.

2. Click **Edit** next to the position in the Experience section of your profile.

3. Click on **Change Company** and begin typing the name of the company.

4. A drop-down menu appears. Click the correct name of the Company and click **Update**.

If you are still unable to edit information on your LinkedIn company page, you can contact Customer Service with your company name. Make sure you have an email address of the company registered to the account.

Company pages, like most social networks now, have a greater emphasis on visual content. So your first step in creating your page is to add a profile image (this could be your logo) and a header image (646x220 pixels).

Your company page has three navigation links at the top:

1. **Home** – this includes your summary or 'About Us' blurb and company information. Include keywords to

help facilitate searches, and make sure you add details of what your company specialises in (in the case of theatre companies, musicals, panto, drama, youth performances etc). The 'Products' section in the sidebar is particularly useful, as it shows the names, details and profile images of people who have recommended specific products and services on your page – a good reason to try to solicit these.

2. **Products** – with your products and services, each with an individual listings complete with a 100 x 80 pixel image, blurb, features and benefits, links to contacts who can provide more information, any special offer details – even embed a You Tube video if you have one. Best of all, it includes a specific weblink for each product or service – essential for driving traffic to your website.

3. **Insights** – a detailed demographic of your followers and company page visitors.

**Create a Linked In Group**

LinkedIn groups are communities of interest within the wider LinkedIn network. Many professional associations have LinkedIn Groups, which are worth joining and contributing to. There are well over a million LinkedIn groups to choose from, so there are bound to be several relevant to you. One of the advantages of groups is that they can help you grow your personal network within those niches that interest you the most, since you can invite members from your group to become contacts.

To create your LinkedIn group, select **Groups** from the Interests drop-down menu at the top of your screen, click **Create a Group** and fill in the details.

Make sure you upload a logo – once people start joining, this 'badge' will show up on their profile, and if your group looks interesting to their contacts, they may click on it and join you too. Add a description with plenty of keywords, include your website, and choose a group type.

You have the option of choosing either:

• **Open Access** – any LinkedIn member may join this group without requiring approval from a manager.

• **Request to join** – users must request to join this group and be approved by a manager.

You should generally choose Open Access to reduce any barriers to building up your membership. Once you have your group set up, you'll need to add content to keep people interested. Group members can start discussions, add news, and post job ads in your group (subject to the settings you choose), but you need to make an effort and do some of the work too. Things you can add include:

• **Discussions** – start a discussion topic, or simply post a message to the discussion area. As administrator, you can also make this a featured item that appears at the top of the list.

• **Links** – attach links to discussions, with a short description.

• **Polls** – with the discussion area you can start a discussion or poll. Ask a question, and specify up to five multiple choice answers. This can be useful to engage your members, and for bits of ad-hoc market research.

Add at least some content before inviting your contacts, even if it is just a welcome message. Don't invite everyone – just those you think might be interested. Promote your group as you would a Facebook group or any new social media channel you start using; put it in your email signature, include a prominent link on your website, mention it in your next email newsletter, tweet about it, etc.

A significant benefit to groups – whether you own or someone else's that you post to – is that the items you submit to them are included in digest emails to group members who accept notofocations from the group. With your own group, you can also Send An Announcement to all the members of your group, which sends an email as well as posting to the discussion area. Use this sparingly (LinkedIn will only allow one of these per week) and think carefully about your message content, as you would with any other mass mailing.

# 22. AND SO IN CLOSING...

I could honestly keep writing about social networking for days and days, new ideas and concepts enter the fray on an almost daily basis.

Your challenge as theatre marketing teams is to keep a vigilant eye out and use any ideas you think may be relevant to you and your group.

Take your time to carefully build social networks that work for you. Don't rush it and spread yourself too thin.

I will be updating the website www.packedrafterspr.co.uk on a regular basis with whatever new ideas I find along the way. I invite you to share anything you find that has worked for you.

Most of all please, please, please, open your minds to the fact that things in the world of theatre are evolving, it's not wrong to try new things. Think about everything you do from the point of view of not just your current audience but the audience you wish would come and see your shows. Make it as easy as possible for people to find you and for people to buy a ticket. Yes you may have to break a few eggs along the way, but the omelette at the end will be so much better!

I wish you and your group all the best. Please keep in touch with me, ask questions, share your success and don't be afraid to take a risk.

# SOCIAL NETWORKS

**Facebook**
www.facebook.com

**Twitter**
www.twitter.com

**Google+**
http://plus.google.com

**Habbo**
www.habbo.com

**LinkedIn**
www.linkedin.com

**Instagram**
http://instagram.com

**Bebo**
www.bebo.com

**Pinterest**
http://pinterest.com

**MySpace**
www.myspace.com

**YouTube**
www.youtube.com

## MAILING LIST SOFTWARE PROVIDERS

Your Mailing List
www.yourmailinglistprovider.com

Constant Contact
www.constantcontact.com

Mail Chimp
www.mailchimp.com

Mailing Manager
www.mailingmanager.co.uk

Dot Mailer
www.dotmailer.co.uk

E-Shot
www.e-shot.net

## WEBSITE SERVICES

Moonfruit
www.moonfruit.com

Wix
www.wix.com

1 and 1
www.1and1.co.uk

Webs
www.webs.com

Weebly
www.weebly.com

Spanglefish
www.spanglefish.com

## ONLINE TICKETING PROVIDERS

Ticket Source
www.ticketsource.co.uk

Positickets
www.positickets.co.uk

Little Box Office
www.littleboxoffice.com

Also by Douglas Mayo

PACKED TO THE RAFTERS

Packed To The Rafters is the ultimate guide to modern PR techniques for amateur and fringe theatre groups. This book makes for essential reading for any PR committee tasked with doing PR for any show for the first time or even those who have done it before and need to brush up on the latest techniques. Having had experience in production and the media, Douglas Mayo guides any potential PR through the process of promoting a show including the press release, email marketing, branding, sponsorship, creative use of photography and social networking.

**Reader's and critical feedback:**
*"Packed to the Rafters" is the most inspirational book I have ever read regarding marketing within amateur theatre. It covered every element of publicity, right from the show being chosen to the opening night and tracking the campaign along the way. I can honestly say my society's production of*

*"Oklahoma" at the Belgrade Theatre in Coventry was the talk of the town thanks to this superb book of knowledge and advice."*
**Adam James Chapman – Marketing & PR Officer**
**Coventry Musical Theatre Society**

*"Packed to the Rafters" became an inspiration to me and I wanted to try out as many of the ideas as I could, I also began to contact people who had a great deal of knowledge in the theatre marketing business who could possibly assist me."*
**Stephen Jenner PR**
**GDS Productions**

*"What a gem of a book. So many facets of good practice – it seems like a total approach to all things necessary to help amateur drama groups get "bums on seats". It is written in an easily digestible style without any dumbing down. I will definitely be recommending this book to my colleagues in other drama groups in the area, as well as implementing these approaches for my own drama group (The Western Players, in Swindon). It is such a valuable resource. Excellent!!"*
**Tony Manders**

*"This wasn't, 'could have been a good book', it was 'an exceptional book', with something for every one connected with the theatre at every level. Having been a writer/director for more than 20 years, I thought I knew it all. Douglas showed me I had a lot to learn – and did. Looking forward to the new publication."*
**Mark Robberts.**

*"With its simple format, page turning content and friendly yet exceptionally informative voice, Packed to the Rafters unravels the mysteries of 21st Century theatre PR. A theatre*

*publicity bible for professionals and amateurs alike, this is surefire must read to secure more bums on seats for your next show!"*

**Skye Crawford, Fringe Review**

*"This book addresses the important issue of getting people through the doors and onto the seats. Douglas obviously knows his stuff and applies professional standards and systems to amateur theatre. Amateur groups need to drag themselves into the 21st century and Douglas's book is just the book to do it."*

**Jane Dickerson. www.amdram.co.uk**

*"This new book by Douglas Mayo is 100% absolutely required reading for all those involved in front of house activities in amateur groups and fringe theatre. Targeted at those who are responsible for marketing and publicity, but also valuable to anybody who interacts with customers, Doug's highly practical advice and sensible suggestions should be devoured and put into practice immediately. Attracting an audience is key to the continuation of any theatre group – this book shows how to do it successfully in today's theatrical environment."*

**David Waters. www.stagescripts.com**

*Packed to the Rafters is a page-turner that will inspire you on to monumental results. Douglas gets to the point, and fast. This book is literally packed to the rafters with insider knowledge, contemporary practices and ideas to get your theatre group and patrons buzzing. Applying just 10% of his advice will surely garner results. Going full throttle with 100% will have your audience queuing round the block! If you're involved in theatre PR in any form, you'd be crazy not to beg, borrow or steal a copy so you can devour every inch.*

**Fourthwall Magazine. www.fourthwallmagazine.co.uk**

"*This book was inspirational! We are a local drama group that has been in existence for over 40 years acknowledged for providing performances of a high standard. I read the book from cover to cover and was really motivated by many of the ideas suggested. We had a newly elected publicity working party. They also read the book, had meetings and as a result we have already implemented some of the ideas. Perhaps the most significant is the on line ticketing system. This is up and running for our next production. We hope to put many of the other suggestions into practice as our season evolves thereby transporting us into the 21st century.*"
**Jan Jones – Chairman Business Committee**

Thorpe Players – Norwich
"*Part of a local operatic society who have been struggling with dwindling audience numbers. This book provides some very useful ideas and tips to help stem that.*"
**Rob Barclay**

"*Loved all the tips and ideas. Thanks for sharing them Will try to include as many as possible. Look forward to the next book*"
**Millenium Stage Productions**

"*As publicity officer for an amateur company I'm sure this book will help me to think outside the traditional publicity box for new successful ideas for marketing and publicising our shows.*"
**Dorothy Lawson**

# The only
# monthly magazine
# passionate
## about
# amateur theatre